Su
of

How Not to Die
Dr. Michael Greger

Conversation Starters

By BookHabits

Please Note: This is an unofficial conversation starters guide. If you have not yet read the original work or would like to read it again, <ins>get the book here.</ins>

We hope you enjoy this complementary guide from BookHabits.
Our mission is to aid readers and reading groups with quality, thought provoking material to in the discovery and discussions on some of today's favorite books.

Tips for Using BookHabits Conversation Starters:

EVERY GOOD BOOK CONTAINS A WORLD FAR DEEPER THAN the surface of its pages. The characters and their world come alive through the words on the pages, yet the characters and its world still live on. Questions herein are designed to bring us beneath the surface of the page and invite us into the world that lives on. These questions can be used to:

- Foster a deeper understanding of the book
- Promote an atmosphere of discussion for groups
- Assist in the study of the book, either individually or corporately
- Explore unseen realms of the book as never seen before

About Us:

THROUGH YEARS OF EXPERIENCE AND FIELD EXPERTISE, from newspaper featured book clubs to local library chapters, *BookHabits* can bring your book discussion to life. Host your book party as we discuss some of today's most widely read books.

Table of Contents

Introducing *How Not to Die*

How Not To Die is written by Dr. Michael Greger (with Gene Stone as co-writer) as a guide to living a better and longer life. It is distilled from over a thousand videos Dr. Greger has done in his website NutritionFacts.org, all focused on healthy eating and nutrition. He has likewise collected compelling evidence of food as medicine and includes this in the book, thus producing a practical guide for readers who want to improve their health through lifestyle and diet.

The book is divided into three parts, the first part focusing on diseases and their plant-based solutions, and the second part is on food and their health benefits. The third and final part of the book lists references used. The first part has 15 chapters that discuss the common ailments that afflict many Americans. Greger writes about the nature and causes of each of these 15 diseases then identifies the foods that are known to alleviate, prevent, reverse or cure them. Among these diseases are diabetes, hypertension, cancers (breast, lung, colorectal, prostate, leukemia), Alzheimer's, and Parkinson's. Based on scientific research, Greger believes that these diseases could be prevented or reversed by eating the right foods. He presents research data on foods that help or worsen these diseases. The second part discusses the ideal diet for people who want to stay healthy and live long. Greger wrote this part to answer the question which he is asked often – "what do you eat everyday?" He enumerates the foods that should be eaten more often, describes the benefits, and the portions recommended. He calls this the "Daily Dozen." He claims that some food groups have nutrients that cannot be found in other foods and therefore cannot be interchangeable. His advise is to make sure that foods from these 12 recommended be eaten everyday to ensure all essential nutrients are present in the body. Greger's main thesis is that eating whole food, plant-based foods and removing processed food and animal products in our diet is the best way to health and longevity. He argues against taking drugs as a solution for health problems, especially if the ailment is related to ones lifestyle. Throughout the book, Greger addresses issues connected to health and nutrition. These include the advantage of eating organic foods, when gluten foods are sometimes better than gluten-free, when and when not to use supplements, and important things to know about GMO foods.

Greger provides footnotes for readers to consult. He cites a lot of clinical evidence and about 3,000 citations, that support his claims on particular foods that help reverse, treat or prevent the diseases. His writing style is easy to read and approachable despite his discussion of technical and scientific terms. He uses stories of personal encounters with patients or family anecdotes to introduce a topic, giving us a closer glimpse of his character and background. His most significant personal anecdote is that of his grandmother who had a heart disease and was sent home by doctors to die because after doing all the operations they could do on her, they could not make her well. She was 65 but went on to live to 96 as a result of a change in diet and lifestyle. He introduces each chapter with a general view of the topic, giving readers a statistical, social and even political aspect of the health issues concerned. His introduction to part 1 discusses the problem and points out the irony in how the problem is not being solved: the primary cause of death in the US is faulty diet but the remedy for this is not being taught in medical schools. In introducing chapter 2, his language is more direct. He cites the practical aspect of the book by pointing out the two tools that readers can use to improve their diet and health: the Traffic Light system and the Daily Dozen. In introducing the whole book, Greger's language is critical and radical. He discusses the problem affecting the US health care system, the defects of the medical training taught in schools, and the things that Big Pharma companies do that don't contribute to healthy practices. He criticizes the corrupting influences in medicine and in in the field of nutrition.

How Not to Die is a *New York Times* Bestseller. The Dalai Lama and Dean Ornish recommend this book as a guide for healthy living. Other reviews cite it for being meticulous in its research, and is well-documented. Though cited by one review for its cherry-picking or selectively choosing facts that support the author's claims, many reviewers call it a comprehensive guide to nutrition, a life changer, and empowering.

Discussion Questions

"Get Ready to Enter a New World"

Tip: Begin with questions dealing with broader issues to ensure ample time for quality discussions. Read through all discussion questions before engaging.

~~~

question 1

The book has three parts--diseases and their plant-based solutions, food and their health benefits, and list of references. Do you think Greger could have added more parts or chapters? Are there other topics you want discussed that were not included? Or is the book comprehensive?

~~~

~~~

question 2

Greger wrote the second part to answer the question which he is asked often – "what do you eat everyday?" He enumerates the foods that should be eaten more often, or what he calls the "Daily Dozen." Would you be interested too to know what he eats? Is the Daily Dozen an achievable diet for you?

~~~

~~~

question 3

Some food groups have nutrients that cannot be found in other foods and therefore cannot be interchangeable. Can you cite some of these food groups? Are there foods that you have not been eating enough of, based on these necessary foods?

~~~

~~~

question 4

He is not in favor of taking drugs as a solution for health problems. He prefers to address the ailment through lifestyle and diet first before considering drugs. Do you agree with his approach? Why? Why not?

~~~

~~~

question 5

He discusses the place of supplements in aiding ones diet. There are some supplements he suggests taking and others he suggests to avoid. Can hou name these necessary and unnecessary supplements? Would you follow his advice?

~~~

~~~

question 6

Greger provides footnotes, clinical evidence and about 3,000 citations, that support his claims on particular foods that help reverse, treat or prevent the diseases. Do you think he did a thorough research on his subject? Would you trust his recommendations because of his research?

~~~

~~~

question 7

His writing is easy to understand despite his discussion of technical and scientific terms. Were you able to understand his explanations of the complex medical and nutrition topics? How does he simplify complex topics?

~~~

~~~

question 8

He uses stories of personal encounters with patients or family anecdotes to introduce a topic, giving us a closer glimpse of his character and background. Which of his stories do you particularly remember? Why?

~~~

~~~

question 9

In his introduction, Greger's language is critical and radical. He discusses the problem affecting the US health care system, the defects of the medical training taught in schools, and the things that Big Pharma companies do that don't contribute to healthy practices. Why do you think he includes this in a book that is largely devoted to diet and health? Do you agree with his views?

~~~

question 10

He points out an irony in the American health situation: the primary cause of death in the US is faulty diet but how to remedy this is not being taught in medical schools. Do you think doctors should learn more about nutrition and the impact of healthy diet on ones wellness? Why do you think they do not focus on this in treating their patients?

~~~

~~~

question 11

The book's main thesis is that eating whole food, plant-based foods and removing processed food and animal products in our diet is the best way to health and longevity. Are you convinced of this? What percentage of your current diet consists of whole and plant-based foods? Of processed food and animal products?

~~~

~ ~ ~

question 12

The book is distilled from over a thousand videos Dr. Greger has done in his website NutritionFacts.org. The videos discuss various issues related to healthy eating and nutrition. Have you seen his website? Do you think this is a site you can go to for health nutrition guidance?

~ ~ ~

~~~

question 13

In chapter 2 he introduces the Traffic Light System designed to help readers choose the proper foods to buy. The green light stands for unprocessed plant foods and the red for ultra-processed foods. Do you find this helpful? Have you started avoiding red light foods?

~~~

~~~

question 14

Greger's research reveals that an average serving of vegetables can cost about four times more than the average serving of junk food but has 24 times more nutrition. Would you rather buy vegetables or junk food? Why?

~~~

~~~

question 15

Greger cites the report by the National Cancer Institute that three out of four Americans don't eat fruit in a given day; nearly nine out of ten don't get the minimum recommended daily intake of vegetables. Are you surprised that so many Americans get cancer? Do you see the connection between diet and cancer as explained by Greger?

~~~

question 16

The Dalai Lama endorsed *How Not to Die* by saying it is a good guide for "maintaining physical health and mental happiness". Would you read the book because of the Dalai Lama's recommendation? Do you think the Dalai Lama practices Greger's recommended diet?

question 17

Dean Ornish, known for his program for reversing heart disease, says the book is "extraordinary and empowering." Do you think the book empowers you? In what way?

~~~

~~~

question 18

BookPage says the book is "meticulously well-documented" and gives evidence for everything. Do you agree with the review? Does being meticulous make the book authoritative?

~~~

~~~

question 19

Goodreads introduces *How Not to Die* as "groundbreaking." The scientific evidence behind it is key to preventing and reversing ailments that lead to deaths. Do you think the scientific evidence presented in the book is its major strength? Do you agree it is groundbreaking?

~~~

~~~

question 20

The Healthline review says Greger's book resorted to cherry-picking or selectively choosing facts that support his claims and ignoring the ones that don't. Do you think the critic has a point here? Would you read and consider the review's arguments?

~~~

Introducing the Author

Michael Greger, M.D., internationally known advocate of nutrition, public health and food safety, became a doctor because of his grandmother. Having seen his grandmother recover from heart disease, even when doctors already gave up on her, Greger was inspired. His grandmother was among the first patients of Nathan Pritikin, a pioneer in advocating heart health through lifestyle change. At that time, doctors had no idea that an end-stage heart disease could be reversed. When he became a doctor, he grew aware of the work of Dean Ornish who did research on preventive medicine. Though his work was published in well-known medical journals, Ornish's discoveries were largely ignored by the medical community. Greger soon realized that there were large forces that influenced medicine apart from science. Medical schools were not teaching enough knowledge about nutrition to students. Diet as a means to treat and reverse diseases was not taught despite presence of evidence.

He made it his life mission to find out more information that was being ignored in medical schools. While practicing medicine, he also spent much time reading about the topic, going through stacks in the basement of Countway Library of Medicine at Harvard. He started giving talks to medical schools, as many as 40 a month, about the power of food. This was with the support of the American Medical Student Association. Greger gave the talks with the intention to inform every medical student. The talks led to the creation of a DVD series called *Latest in Clinical Nutrition* which is now on its 30th volume. The proceeds of the DVD sales, his talks, and book sales including this book, all go directly to charity. To continue the growing amount of work, NutritionFacts.org was soon set up through the help of Canadian philanthropist Jesse Rasch. The website has a compilation of videos and articles on nutrition topics which Greger covered through the years. He posts new material everyday and all of these are for free. It is his labor of love.

Greger thinks that in the advent of the internet age, people can empower themselves by having access to knowledge about health. He continues his work today by employing a team of researchers and numerous volunteers who help him dig information. He lives near the world's largest medical library, the National Library of Medicine where he and his team go through thousands of medical literature related to nutrition.

Greger, a graduate of Cornell University, is also the health director of the Humane Society of the United States. He has three cats and a dog. In addition to his work as a physician and health advocate, he also actively promotes the welfare of animals.

In concluding his book, Greger tells the story of his friend Art, owner of a successful natural foods business. Despite his healthy diet and regimen, Art died at the age of 46. The cause of death, it turned out, was carbon monoxide poisoning. Greger says that though healthy living ensures us to live well, we could just get hit by a bus. That is why we need to take care of ourselves, make each day count, enjoy the air, laugh and love.

Fireside Questions

"What would you do?"

Tip: These questions can be a fun exercise as it spurs creativity among the readers by allowing alternate scene endings and "if this was you" questions.

question 21

Greger was inspired by his grandmother who recovered from a terminal heart disease when doctors already gave up on her. He decided to become a doctor. What about his grandmother's case that inspired him? Do you think his grandmother would be proud of him if she sees her grandson today a leading advocate of food as medicine?

~~~

~~~

question 22

Greger realized that medical schools were not teaching enough knowledge about nutrition and diet as a means to treat and reverse diseases. This was despite presence of evidence. Why do you think medical schools do not give attention to the importance of diet? Do you find it strange that diet is excluded by medical doctors as a form of treatment?

~~~

~ ~ ~

question 23

Greger wanted to inform every medical student and started giving talks to medical schools, as many as 40 a month, about the power of food and its medical use. Why do you think he worked hard to inform medical students? What drives him to do this?

~ ~ ~

~~~

question 24

With NutritionFacts.org, Greger thinks that in the advent of the internet age, people can empower themselves by having access to knowledge about health. Do you think he is dispossessing doctors of their power and authority over sick people? Do you think this is a good thing?

~~~

~~~

question 25

He calls his work a labor of love. Would you agree
with him? Is there anything he had to sacrifice to
be able to do his work?

~~~

~~~

question 26

Greger's inspiration in becoming a doctor was his grandmother who survived a supposedly terminal heart disease. If she did not survive the disease, do you think Greger would be a doctor today? If no, what do you think would he be?

~~~

~~~

question 27

The book has 3,000 citations and is well-researched. If Greger did not bother to cite his references, do you think it would be credible? Would you still like the book?

~~~

~~~

question 28

He tells stories about himself and his encounters with patients to illustrate some points in the book. If these stories were not included in the book, how different would it be? Would you still have a better impression of him as a person?

~~~

~~~

question 29

The book is readable despite its medical and scientific terms. If his language is more formal, like a professor giving lectures, would it be as interesting? Would it be more credible?

~~~

~ ~ ~

question 30

Greger was able to put up NutritionFacts.org through the help of a philanthropist who believed in healthy food as medicine. If there is no NutritionFacts.org, would there be less knowledge about food and nutrition issues? Would there be an alternative website where people can access the kind of information he produces?

~ ~ ~

Quiz Questions

"Ready to Announce the Winners?"

Tip: Create a leaderboard and track scores to see who gets the most correct answers. Winners required. Prizes optional.

~~~

quiz question 1

True or False: The first part of the book focuses on 15 diseases and the foods known to cure, alleviate, reverse or prevent them.

~~~

quiz question 2

The second part of the book is written by Greger to answer the question _____, a question he is often asked.

~~~

quiz question 3

He enumerates 12 foods that should be eaten daily.
He calls these foods the _____.

~ ~ ~

~~~

quiz question 4

True or False: In the book, Greger presents evidence to support his claim that eating whole food, plant-based foods and removing processed food and animal products in our diet is the best way to health and longevity.

~~~

quiz question 5

True or False: In chapter 2 he introduces the Traffic Light System designed to help readers choose the proper foods to buy. The _____ light stands for unprocessed plant foods and the red for ultra-processed foods.

~~~

quiz question 6

True or False: The book is distilled from over a thousand videos Dr. Greger has done in his website NutritionFacts.org.

~~~

quiz question 7

True or False: The primary cause of death in the US is faulty diet according to Greger. Medical schools are teaching students how to have a healthy diet in order to prevent these deaths.

quiz question 8

. Greger dedicates the book to his _____. He became a doctor because of her.

~~~

quiz question 9

As a young doctor, Greger was aware of the work of _____ who did research on diet and preventive medicine. Though this doctor's work was published in well-known medical journals, his discoveries were largely ignored by the medical community.

~ ~ ~

quiz question 10

True or False: Greger realized that medical schools were not teaching enough knowledge about nutrition and diet as a means to treat and reverse diseases.

quiz question 11

True or False: Greger believes that his website NutritionFacts.org, can help people empower themselves by having access to knowledge about health and nutrition.

~~~

quiz question 12

True or False: Greger has three dogs and a cat. He actively promotes the welfare of animals.

~~~

Quiz Answers

1. True
2. What do you eat everyday?
3. Daily Dozen
4. True
5. green
6. True
7. False
8. grandmother
9. Dean Ornish
10. True
11. True
12. False

Ways to Continue Your Reading

EVERY month, our team runs through a wide selection of books to pick the best titles for readers and reading groups, and promotes these titles to our thousands of readers – sometimes with free downloads, sale dates, and additional brochures.

If you have not yet read the original work or would like to read it again, get the book here.

Want to register yourself or a book group? It's free and takes 1-click.

Register here.

On the Next Page...

Please write us your reviews! Any length would be fine but we'd appreciate hearing you more! We'd be SO grateful.

Till next time,

BookHabits

"Loving Books is Actually a Habit"